21st
Century
Skills Library

ANIMAL INVADERS

EMERALD ASH BORER

Susan H. Gray

Cherry Lake Publishing
Ann Arbor, Michigan

Published in the United States of America by Cherry Lake Publishing
Ann Arbor, MI
www.cherrylakepublishing.com

Content Adviser: Anand B. Persad, PhD, BCE, Regional Technical Adviser/Lecturer
Entomology, ISA Certified Arborist, The Davey Institute, Kent, Ohio

Please note: Our map is as up-to-date as possible at the time of publication.

Photo Credits: Cover and pages 1, 4, 6, 8, 9, 11, 12, and 25, © David Cappaert, Michigan
State University, Bugwood.org; page 13, © Brian Sullivan, USDA, APHIS, PPQ,
Bugwood.org; page 15, © Pennsylvania Department of Conservation and Natural
Resources-Forestry Archive, Pennsylvania Department of Conservation and Natural
Resources, Bugwood.org; page 18, © Joseph O'Brien, USDA Forest Service, Bugwood.
org; pages 20, 22, and 26, © David Cappaert

Map by XNR Productions Inc.

Library of Congress Cataloging-in-Publication Data
Gray, Susan H.
 Emerald ash borer / by Susan H. Gray.
   p. cm.—(Animal invaders)
 ISBN-13: 978-1-60279-112-1
 ISBN-10: 1-60279-112-0
 1. Emerald ash borer—Juvenile literature. I. Title. II. Series.
 QL596.B8G73 2008
 595.76'3—dc22   2007034973

*Cherry Lake Publishing would like to acknowledge the work of
The Partnership for 21st Century Skills.
Please visit www.21stcenturyskills.org for more information.*

TABLE OF CONTENTS

CHAPTER ONE

EAT AND GO

The emerald ash borer larva zigzags under tree bark.

The **larva** eats a tiny bit and then scoots forward. It lives just beneath the bark of an ash tree. Its body is tightly sandwiched between the bark and a thick layer of wood. It barely has room to move. Its world is completely dark and almost silent.

The surroundings are not comfortable. But the food supply for this young emerald ash borer is plentiful. Water and **nutrients** are to the larva's right and left, above its body and below it. All the larva has to do is to keep eating and scooting forward.

And scooting and eating it does, day after day, chewing a tunnel as it goes. This continues for weeks. Finally, the larva stops, changes into an adult beetle, and drills, or bores, its way out of the tree.

Learning & Innovation Skills

It's only a little green beetle, no bigger than a penny. How can the emerald ash borer be such an enormous pest? It is a pest if it's an invasive **species**. A species is a particular kind of plant or animal. And an invasive species is one that has moved into a new area and has taken over. In its new home, an invasive species may have no natural enemies, and it can grow out of control. Its numbers will increase, and perhaps little can be done to stop it.

Human activity usually brings in invasive species. People can carry in these plants or animals on ships, in crates of fruit, and even in boxes of clothing. The emerald ash borer probably came to North America in wooden crates from Asia. Since then, its numbers have grown.

Now, millions of emerald ash borers are in North America, and the insect has become a pest. Can you think of any way shipping companies could have kept these beetles out?

CHAPTER TWO

A BORING LIFE

Adult emerald ash borers have three main body parts and two sets of wings.

The adult emerald ash borer is a small, slender beetle. It is named for its emerald green color and its behavior. The borer spends its whole life inside, on, and around ash trees. It also has a habit of boring holes into and out of those trees.

Like other beetles, its body has three main parts—the head, **thorax**, and **abdomen**. The small head has two large black- or copper-colored eyes. On the thorax are three pairs of legs and two pairs of wings. The outer wings are a bright, metallic green. The inner wings beneath these are more delicate.

When the wings are spread, you can see a shiny, reddish-purple abdomen. Adults are about 0.3 to 0.6 inch (0.8 to 1.4 centimeters) in length.

The emerald ash borer spends most of its life just beneath the bark of the ash

The emerald ash borer is a kind of beetle. And beetles are types of insects. Like all insects, the emerald ash borers have three body parts, six legs, and **antennae**.

Like all beetles, emerald ash borers also have body parts called **elytra**. You have probably noticed these on beetles around your home. The elytra are hard wings that fold down to cover the back of the beetle. Beneath them are light, lacy wings. When the beetle flies, it holds its elytra out to the sides for balance. The delicate wings underneath do the flying. In addition to aiding balance, what other purpose might elytra serve?

Emerald ash borer eggs are about 0.04 inch (1 millimeter) wide.

tree. Only as an adult does it come out and begin to fly around. Males and females mate in the spring, about 7 to 10 days after boring their way out of the trees. The female lays her eggs a little more than a week later.

She lays about 70 to 90 tiny, white eggs on the bark of the ash tree. A week or so later, the eggs hatch. Small, creamy-white larvae creep out. They look nothing like

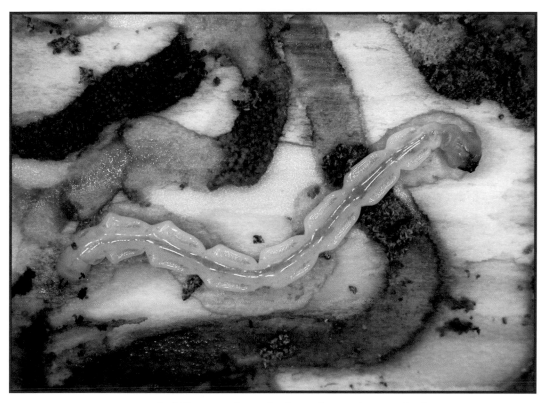

A nearly full-grown larva feeds on the cambium. That's the thin tissue layer under a tree's inner bark.

their parents. Right away, they begin to bore their way through the bark and into the tree. They are heading straight for their food supply.

Under the tree's outer bark is a layer of tissue called the inner bark. Food for the tree flows through tiny tubes in this layer. Beneath this is a thin tissue layer called the **cambium**.

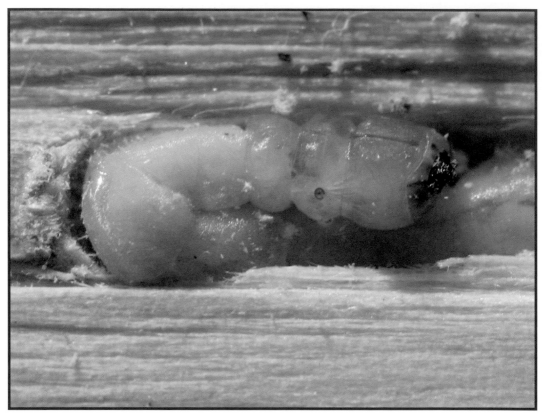

This larva is becoming a pupa. The next stage is adulthood.

Just under the cambium is a layer called the **sapwood**. Tubes in the sapwood carry water and nutrients up from the roots to the leaves.

When the larvae bore into the tree, they are going straight for the inner bark, cambium, and sapwood. The inner bark and sapwood are loaded with water and nutrients. The cambium is where the larvae dig their tunnels. They stay here for weeks, stealing nutrients from the tree's own food supply.

Larvae spend the whole summer just eating and growing. The largest ones grow to be about 1.3 inches (3.2 cm) long—longer even than the adult beetle. Larvae bodies are flat with many parts. As the larvae feed, they scoot forward, forming tunnels. They sometimes double back, creating Z- and S-shaped tunnels. Because they are hidden beneath the bark, no one knows they are there.

The larvae spend the winter at the end of one of the tunnels. In the early spring, they enter the next stage and become **pupae**. The pupae look like young, soft-bodied adults. They are white and then darken.

The pupae continue to develop, and their bodies and wings harden. In time, they become adult beetles. They bore D-shaped holes in the bark while exiting.

Sometimes, when the emerald ash borer senses danger, it will drop to the ground and lie completely still. How could such behavior help the borer survive?

Emerald ash borers drill D-shaped holes to exit the tree..

The adults feed on leaves of the ash tree. Most do not fly farther than 0.5 mile (0.8 kilometer) from home. Males live about two weeks, and females live three. In that short period, they mate and lay eggs, starting the cycle again.

CHAPTER THREE

INVADING BEETLES

*After exiting the tree, the adult emerald ash borer feeds on leaves.
The feeding it does as a larva is what damages the ash tree.*

Years ago, the emerald ash borer lived only in China, Russia, Japan, and some other Asian countries. In 2002, the beetle was discovered in Detroit, Michigan. Scientists believe that the ash borer probably arrived several years earlier but no one noticed them.

Michigan is thousands of miles away from China and Russia. Emerald ash borers usually do not fly far from home. They could not have flown all the way to North America! How did they get there?

The borers probably came on cargo ships from Asia. They might have been hidden inside the lumber used to make crates or tucked away in packing material. As larvae or pupae, they could have remained hidden and unnoticed for the entire trip.

Ships reaching North America often sail down the Saint Lawrence River. This river is a busy waterway leading to the Great Lakes. Ports in both the United States and Canada receive shipments along the way. Four of the Great Lakes border Michigan. So this state sees plenty of cargo ships.

After arriving in North America, the ash borers left their old homes and entered their new ones. In Michigan, they

*Underneath the bark, emerald ash borer larvae
are at work destroying the tree.*

crept out, found plenty of ash trees, and settled in. For the

first few years, there were so few emerald ash borers that

no one discovered them. These beetles sometimes take

several years to damage a tree. It's possible not to notice

that they are hard at work beneath the bark.

By the time someone had discovered them, it was too late. The beetles had already begun to spread. Now they are eating through trees all throughout Michigan. They are also in Indiana, Ohio, Illinois, Pennsylvania, and Maryland. These invading insects could arrive almost anywhere ash trees grow. In Canada, they are spreading north from southern Ontario.

In 2003, the emerald ash borers made it to Virginia. But quick-thinking individuals got rid of the pests. Earlier that year, a plant store, or nursery, in Michigan had sent ash trees filled with emerald ash borers to another store in Maryland, which sold some of the trees to schools in Virginia. Government workers in Virginia noticed the trees had emerald ash borers and immediately took action.

They removed and burned all of the infested trees. They also removed and burned more than 200 other ash trees that were within 0.5 mile (0.8 km) of the infested ones. The government workers handled the problem before the borers could spread. Several years later, no one has reported any emerald ash borers in Virginia.

CHAPTER FOUR

BEETLES WORKING IN SECRET

*Damage to ash trees from emerald ash borers
includes splits in the protective bark.*

Ash trees, like all kinds of trees, sometimes get diseases
or come under attack. Extremely small worms can
destroy their roots. Ash plant bugs, other kinds of
beetles, and mites can eat their leaves. Deer chew on the

tender branches of young trees. And rabbits and beavers sometimes gnaw the bark of **seedlings**. Ash trees certainly have their share of problems. Why isn't the emerald ash borer just one more problem?

Emerald ash borers are a serious problem because they cause damage so quickly and so secretly. The beetle's tiny eggs are almost impossible to see. As soon as the eggs hatch, the larvae disappear into the tree. There, under the bark, they suck away the tree's food.

Within a year, the upper branches begin to die. The bark may split and fall off in chunks. Within three years, the tree could be dead. In the meantime, the beetles have multiplied and moved on to other trees.

This is what happened in Michigan. Once people realized the borers had invaded, it was too late. Thousands of ash trees were dead or dying. By then, the emerald ash borers were there to stay.

Healthy ash trees are tall and leafy all the way to the top.

Experts believe there are about 8 billion ash trees in the forests of the United States. These trees are valuable for several reasons. People enjoy them for their shade and beauty in yards, in parks, and along city streets. The trees provide homes for birds and squirrels. Birds feed on their seeds, and insects eat their leaves.

People also prize the sturdy wood of the ash tree. Ash wood can withstand sudden pressure without breaking. Baseball bats, hockey sticks, and boat paddles are made of ash for this reason. Chairs, tables, dressers, and other pieces of furniture are also made of ash.

Ash trees are hardy. They grow in the cold regions of Canada and in warm, damp areas of Florida. They grow at sea level as well as high in the mountains. On hillsides, the trees help to keep soil from washing away. And, as the emerald ash borer spreads, more and more of these important trees are in danger.

Life & Career Skills

Asia is the native home of the emerald ash borer. And plenty of ash trees grow in Asia. But it seems that the ash borers do not harm ash trees there as badly as they do in North America. Scientists have discovered that the Asian trees have a resistance to the ash borers. The borers infest the trees, but the trees usually do not die. Perhaps this is because the trees and borers have lived together for many years. Over time, the trees have developed a system for surviving the insect's attacks. Studying the Asian trees may help scientists learn how to save the North American trees.

CHAPTER FIVE

SPORES AND MORE

A worker injects chemicals into an ash tree trunk to protect it from emerald ash borers. This method doesn't work if the tree is already dying.

Many people are working to solve the problem of the emerald ash borer. They have come up with several solutions. These solutions include killing the beetles, setting up **quarantines**, and destroying the ash trees.

Killing the beetles usually involves using a chemical. Experts can inject chemicals that are poisonous to larvae into the ground near an ash tree. The tree roots draw up the chemicals, along with water and nutrients. The chemicals, water, and nutrients move up the tree's transport system to the branches and leaves. When the larvae feed on materials passing through the transport system, they take in the chemicals and die.

There are problems with this method, however. The injected or sprayed poisons may also kill earthworms and honeybees. Birds might eat poisoned worms or insects and die as well. Scientists are working on ways to limit the negative effects on other species.

Some people have tried spraying tree trunks with **fungal spores**. These are tiny cells that may grow into a new fungus. A fungus is an **organism** that often causes disease in plants and animals.

One particular fungus infects and kills emerald ash borers. The tree spray is meant to kill the adults. As soon as the adults break out from under the bark, they come in contact with the spores. The borers die from a fungal disease before they can mate and lay eggs.

Quarantines are helping in some places. Where the borers are a big problem, state governments have made laws to keep people from spreading them. Quarantine laws are meant to stop human activities that help emerald ash borers spread more quickly.

Laws now prohibit campers from bringing their own firewood to a campsite. Laws also keep people from going from town to town selling firewood. They prohibit nurseries from selling ash trees to people in other states. These laws are keeping people from moving the infested trees and logs and spreading the emerald ash borers to new places.

Spraying chemicals onto ash trees can help get rid of ash borers, but the poisons can also hurt or kill other animals.

Emerald ash borers have caused forests to be turned into wood chips.

In some places, burning a wide band of trees seems
to be the best way to control the borers. Before a burn,
experts first find an area of infested trees. They next

determine a line where the infested trees stop and the healthy trees start. Then they burn all the healthy trees in a wide path outside of that line. The ash borers inside the line have nowhere to go and they die out.

Probably the best solution is to use several methods at once. The emerald ash borers continue to be an invasive species, however. Perhaps one day they will no longer be animal invaders in North America.

In the last half of the 20th century, people recognized that the problem of invasive species was a global issue. They saw that these species created problems around the world and they needed to take action. Eventually, a group of experts came together to discuss solutions. This group of experts from more than 40 countries is called the Invasive Species Specialist Group. They are working on ways to control invasive species around the world.

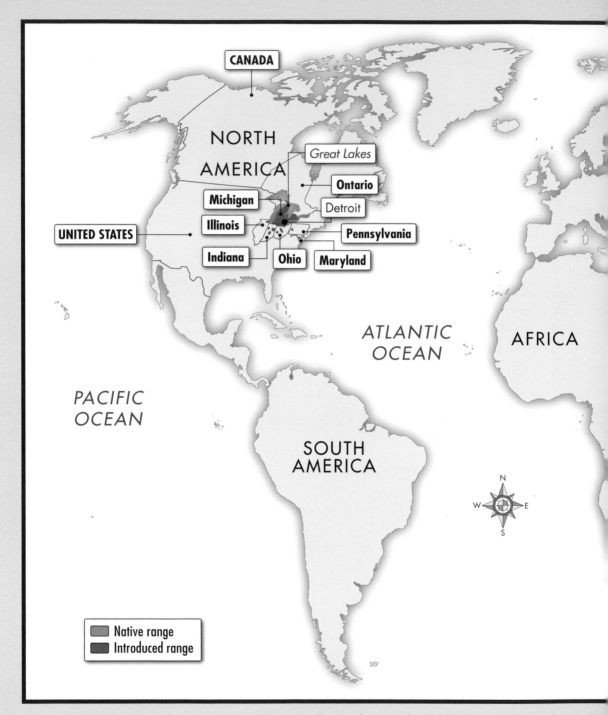

CANADA

NORTH
AMERICA

Great Lakes

Ontario

Detroit

Michigan

Illinois

UNITED STATES

Pennsylvania

Indiana

Ohio

Maryland

ATLANTIC
OCEAN

AFRICA

PACIFIC
OCEAN

SOUTH
AMERICA

N
W E
S

Native range
Introduced range

This map shows where in the world the emerald ash borer

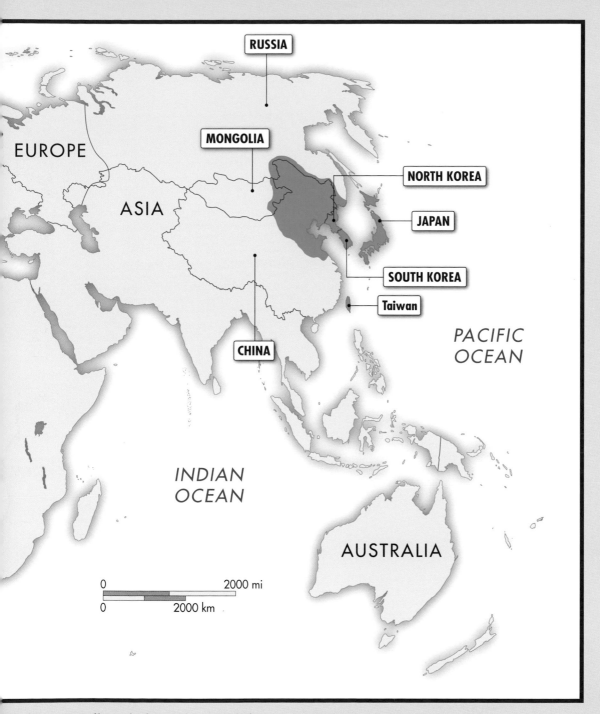

lives naturally and where it has invaded.

Glossary

abdomen (AB-duh-muhn) the last section of an insect's body

antennae (an-TEN-eye) feelers on the head of an insect

cambium (KAM-bee-um) a thin tissue layer under the inner bark of a tree

elytra (EL-ih-truh) hard wings that fold down to cover the back of a beetle

fungal spores (FUNG-ul SPORZ) tiny cells that develop into a new fungus, a type of organism that often causes disease in plants and animals (mushrooms and molds are fungi)

larva (LAR-vuh) an early, wormlike stage in the life of many animals; more than one larva are called larvae (LAR-vee)

nutrients (NOO-tree-uhntz) substances in food that keep plants and animals healthy and strong

organism (OR-guh-niz-uhm) an individual living thing, such as a plant, animal, or fungus

pupae (PYOO-pee) insects at the nonfeeding stage between larvae and adults

quarantines (KWAR-uhn-teenz) periods during which no movement of people or objects is permitted in order to stop the spread of a problem or disease

sapwood (SAP-wud) the layer beneath the cambium that carries water and nutrients from the roots to the leaves of a tree

seedings (SEED-leengz) very young plants that have grown from seeds

species (SPEE-sheez) a group of similar plants or animals

thorax (THOR-aks) the middle part of an insect's three-part body

FOR MORE INFORMATION

Books

MacMillan, Dianne M. *Life in a Deciduous Forest*. Minneapolis: Lerner Publications, 2003.

May, Suellen. *Invasive Terrestrial Animals*. New York: Chelsea House, 2007.

Squire, Ann O. *Beetles*. Danbury, CT: Children's Press, 2004.

Web Sites

U.S. Department of Agriculture (USDA) Forest Service: Emerald Ash Borer
www.emeraldashborer.info
For facts and photos, updated maps, and frequently asked
questions about the emerald ash borer

USDA National Agricultural Library: Emerald Ash Borer
www.invasivespeciesinfo.gov/animals/eab.shtml
To read recent related news articles and locate images of the emerald ash borer in action

INDEX

ABOUT THE AUTHOR

Susan H. Gray has a master's degree in zoology. She has written more than 70 science and reference books for children, and especially loves writing about animals. Gray also likes to garden and play the piano. She lives in Cabot, Arkansas, with her husband, Michael, and many pets.